$22.78
11-04

Nathan Hale

A Buddy Book
by
Christy DeVillier

ABDO
Publishing Company

VISIT US AT
www.abdopub.com

Published by ABDO Publishing Company, 4940 Viking Drive, Suite 622, Edina, Minnesota 55435. Copyright © 2004 by Abdo Consulting Group, Inc. International copyrights reserved in all countries. No part of this book may be reproduced in any form without written permission from the publisher.

Printed in the United States.

Edited by: Michael P. Goecke
Contributing Editor: Matt Ray
Image Research: Deborah Coldiron
Graphic Design: Jane Halbert
Cover Photograph: Library of Congress
Interior Photographs/Illustrations: Hulton Archives, Library of Congress, North Wind

Library of Congress Cataloging-in-Publication Data

DeVillier, Christy, 1971–
   Nathan Hale / Christy DeVillier.
     v. cm. — (First biographies)
   Includes index.
   Contents: Who is Nathan Hale?—Growing up—School life—Teaching—Joining the Revolution—Fighting the British—A dangerous job—Famous last words.
   ISBN 1-59197-513-1
   1. Hale, Nathan, 1755–1776—Juvenile literature. 2. United States—History—Revolution, 1775–1783—Secret Service—Juvenile literature. 3. Spies—United States—Biography—Juvenile literature. 4. Soldiers—United States—Biography—Juvenile literature. [1. Hale, Nathan, 1755–1776. 2. Spies. 3. United States—History—Revolution, 1775–1783—Secret service.] I. Title.

E280.H2D48 2004
973.3'85'092—dc21
[B]
                                                    2003052262

Table Of Contents

Who Is Nathan Hale? 4

Growing Up 6

School Life 8

Teaching 12

Joining The Revolution 16

Fighting The British 20

A Dangerous Job 22

Famous Last Words 26

Important Dates 30

Important Words 31

Web Sites 31

Index 32

Who Is Nathan Hale?

Nathan Hale was a great American Patriot. He fought in the Revolutionary War. Nathan Hale died for his country in 1776.

Today, Nathan Hale's words are famous. People remember him for saying, "I only regret that I have but one life to lose for my country."

Nathan Hale is a Revolutionary War hero.

Growing Up

Nathan Hale was born on June 6, 1755. He had 11 brothers and sisters. They lived on a farm in Coventry, Connecticut. Back then, Connecticut was a colony. Britain ruled the colonies.

Richard Hale was Nathan's father. Nathan's mother was Elizabeth Strong. They were Puritans. The Puritans believed in God.

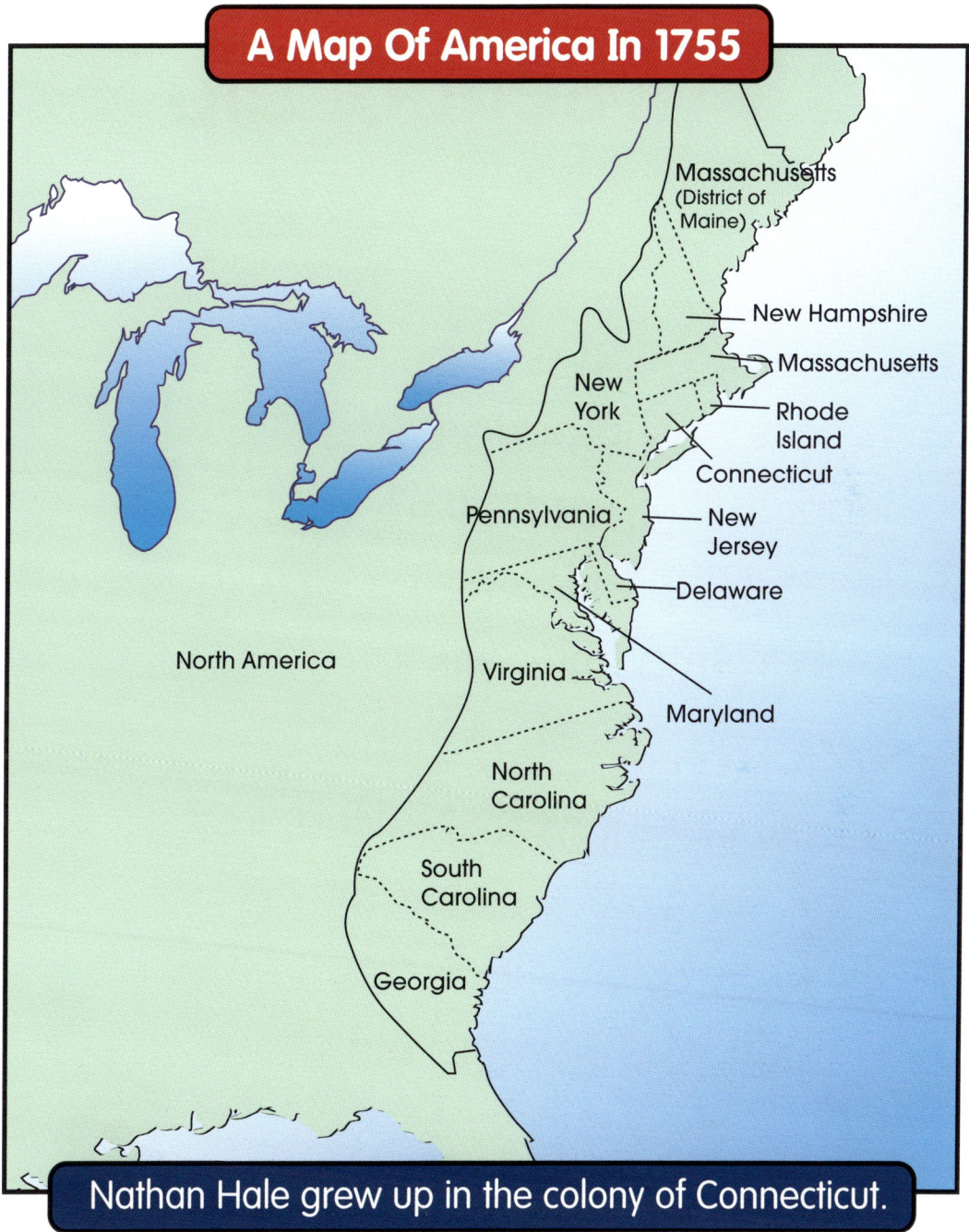

School Life

Nathan's parents believed school was important. They wanted Nathan to study and learn. Nathan learned a lot with help from a tutor. His tutor was Reverend Joseph Huntington.

Nathan enjoyed studying. In 1769, he went to Yale College with his brother, Enoch. At this time, Nathan was 14 years old.

Tutors teach one student at a time.

Yale College in 1718

Nathan enjoyed being a student. He took part in sports and plays. Nathan and Enoch joined a secret club for boys, too.

Nathan and Enoch lived in a building at Yale called New College. Today, New College is called Connecticut Hall. It still stands today at Yale.

Connecticut Hall at Yale University

Teaching

Nathan graduated from Yale College in 1773. He became a schoolteacher. His first teaching job was in East Haddam, Connecticut.

A few months later, Nathan moved to New London, Connecticut. New London was a city on the coast. He began teaching at the Union School.

> Nathan Hale moved from East Haddam to New London in 1773.

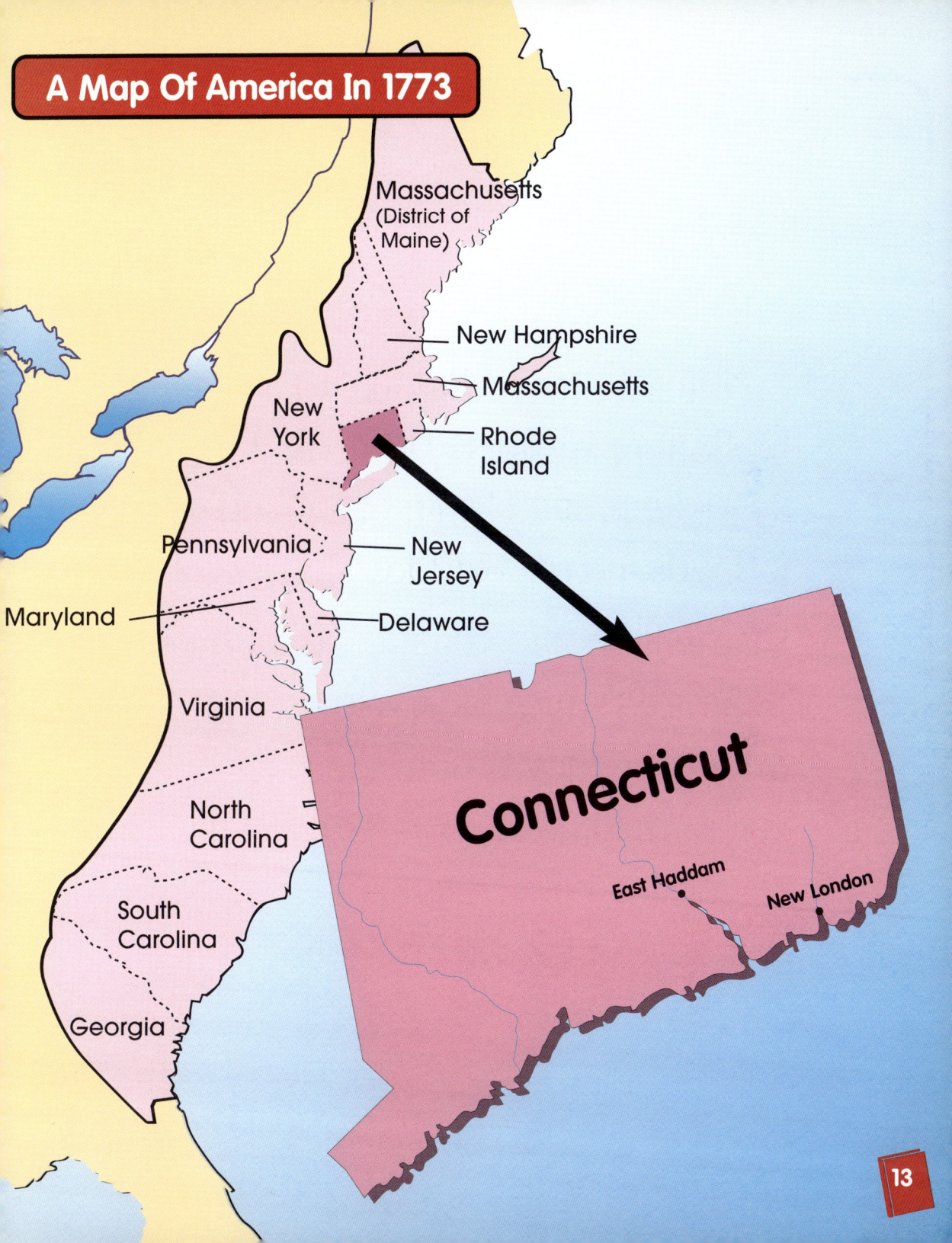

Nathan enjoyed teaching. His students thought he was a good teacher. In 1774, he taught a class for young women. Back then, few women went to college. Nathan believed that college was important for women, too.

Girton College was one of the first colleges for women.

Joining The Revolution

Over time, many colonists became unhappy with Britain. They complained about British taxes. Some colonists wanted to be free of British rule. They wanted to form their own country.

In 1775, Americans began fighting the British. This was the beginning of the Revolutionary War.

Fights broke out between the British and the unhappy colonists.

In July 1775, Nathan got a letter from his friend, Benjamin Tallmadge. Tallmadge believed Americans should fight for their freedom. His letter helped Nathan decide to fight for America.

Nathan quit his teaching job. He joined the Continental army as a first lieutenant. Their leader was General George Washington. Washington later became the first president of the United States.

General George Washington was the leader of the Continental army.

Fighting The British

In 1776, Nathan became an army captain. He led his company to New York. They defended forts during the Battle of Long Island. The Continental army lost this battle. The British took over western Long Island.

General Washington needed help to defend Manhattan, New York. He gathered a special group of soldiers. These skilled soldiers were called the New England Rangers. Nathan was chosen to lead a company of Rangers. This was a big honor for Nathan.

A Dangerous Job

General Washington needed to know Britain's plans. He wondered where Britain would attack. Washington needed a soldier to spy on the British army.

Spying was a dangerous job. Nathan knew the British commonly killed spies. But Nathan told Washington he would do it.

Nathan Hale agreed to become a spy for George Washington.

Nathan dressed up as a schoolteacher. He went to Long Island, New York, where British troops were. Nathan gathered information. While he was there, the British attacked Manhattan.

Nathan Hale tried to return to his army on September 21, 1776. But the British caught him. They discovered he was an American spy.

British soldiers caught Nathan Hale.

Famous Last Words

The British put Nathan Hale to death on September 22, 1776. Before Nathan died, he made a speech.

A British captain told William Hull about Nathan's last words. William Hull was a friend of Nathan's. His book records Nathan's last words as:

"I only regret that I have but one life to lose for my country."

Nathan Hale said his famous last words before dying in 1776.

Nathan Hale bravely died for his country. He is an American hero.

Today, there are statues of Nathan Hale in many United States cities. One stands in New York's City Hall. Another is at Yale University. Washington, D.C., has a statue of Nathan Hale, too. Americans have not forgotten Nathan Hale's patriotic spirit.

This statue of Nathan Hale stands in Chicago, Illinois.

Important Dates

June 6, 1755 Nathan Hale is born.

1769 Nathan starts school at Yale College.

1773 Nathan graduates from Yale College. He becomes a schoolteacher.

1774 Nathan joins the militia in New London, Connecticut.

April 1775 The first battle of the American Revolution takes place.

July 1775 Nathan joins the Continental army led by George Washington.

July 4, 1776 American leaders sign the Declaration of Independence.

August 27, 1776 Americans lose the Battle of Long Island.

September 1776 Nathan leads a company of New England Rangers.

September 21, 1776 The British catch Nathan and discover he is a spy.

September 22, 1776 Nathan Hale bravely dies for his country. He was 21 years old.

Important Words

colony a settlement. Colonists are the people who live in a colony.

patriot someone who loves their country.

Revolutionary War the war Americans fought to win their freedom from Britain.

spy to secretly watch what others are doing.

tax money charged by a city or country.

tutor a teacher who teaches one student at a time.

Web Sites

To learn more about Nathan Hale, visit ABDO Publishing Company on the World Wide Web at www.abdopub.com. Web sites about Nathan Hale are featured on our Book Links page. These links are routinely monitored and updated to provide the most current information available.

Index

Battle of Long Island **20, 30**

Britain **6, 16, 22**

colony **6, 7**

Connecticut **6, 7, 13**

Continental army **18, 19, 20, 30**

Coventry, CT **6**

East Haddam, CT **12, 13**

Hale, Enoch **8, 10, 11**

Hale, Richard **6, 8**

Hull, William **26**

Huntington, Reverend Joseph **8**

Long Island, NY **20, 24**

Manhattan, NY **21, 24**

New England Rangers **21, 30**

New London, CT **12, 13, 30**

patriot **4, 28**

Puritans **6**

Revolutionary War **4, 5, 16**

Strong, Elizabeth **6, 8**

Tallmadge, Benjamin **18**

taxes **16**

Union School **12**

Washington, General George **18, 19, 21, 22, 23, 30**

Yale College **8, 10, 11, 12, 28, 30**

32